MW00979331

S.M.A.R.T.E.R. STEPS™ GUIDE TO CREATING Smarter IEP GOALS

S.M.A.R.T.E.R. STEPS™ GUIDE TO CREATING Smarter IEP GOALS

7 Step Prompting System for Developing Compliant Goals

KELLY OTT, MED, MHS, CCC-SLP
LARA WAKEFIELD, PHD, CCC-SLP

2016

© 2016 S.M.A.R.T.E.R. STEPS™ Kelly Ott and Lara Wakefield

ALL RIGHTS RESERVED. This book contains material protected under the International and Federal Copyright Laws and Treaties. Any unauthorized reprint or use of this material is strictly prohibited. Permission is granted for the user to reproduce, for instructional use only, the workbook pages in the appendices. No other portion of this book may be reproduced or transmitted in any form or by any means, electronic or mechanical, including photocopying, recording, filming, or by any information storage and/or retrieval system without express written permission from the Author/Publisher.

Printed in the United States of America

First Printing 2016

ISBN 1536816248
ISBN 13: 9781536816242
Library of Congress Control Number: 2016912440
CreateSpace Independent Publishing Platform
North Charleston, South Carolina

S.M.A.R.T.E.R. STEPS™
98 Corporate Lake Drive
Columbia, MO 65203

www.smartersteps.com

Ordering Information:
Special discounts are available on quantity purchases by corporations, associations, educators, and others. For details, contact the publisher at above listed address.

U.S. trade bookstores and wholesalers: Please contact S.M.A.R.T.E.R. STEPS™ at team@smartersteps.com.

Dedication

This book is dedicated to every member of the IEP team who serves children with special needs. This includes college professors, mentors, special education teachers, administrators, speech language pathologists, occupational therapists, physical therapists, counselors, and parents. You are the driving force for success of your students and play a vital role in their future. Your wisdom, passion, and dedication is an inspiration to us all.

About the Authors

Kelly Ott

Kelly Ott, MEd, MHS, CCC-SLP, has over 20 years of experience in various roles as an administrator, regular educator, and speech-language pathologist. She has served students from preschool through high school with a wide range of special education needs. She is currently in private practice and contracts with public schools. Several national and state organizations have invited Kelly to present on higher order thinking skills, compliant IEP goals, and collaborative approaches to learning. Kelly's diverse experiences have allowed her to serve in several roles on the IEP team and she brings these multiple perspectives to professional development trainings.

Lara Wakefield

Lara Wakefield, PhD, CCC-SLP, has over 20 years of experience as a speech-language pathologist, researcher, and parent advocate. Lara is in private practice and assists parents with special education advocacy in 27 districts in mid-Missouri. She has presented nationally on the topics of collaborative models of intervention, compliant IEP goals, and evidence-based approaches. Lara is the recipient of three U.S. Department of Education grants and three Missouri Department of Education grants. She helps professionals and parents understand research and legal jargon in a meaningful way as it applies to special education.

Contents

Preface

S.M.A.R.T.E.R. STEPS™ is a professional development company special-izing in best practices related to special education mandates and research. Kelly Ott and Lara Wakefield developed S.M.A.R.T.E.R. STEPS™ for both professionals and families in order to assist them with the struggles of the Individualized Education Program (IEP) process. This guide was designed to introduce an easier and less stressful way to write legally compliant IEP goals.

One of our students asked, "What good is this diploma if I don't have the knowledge to back it up?" Schools, educators, parents, and students tend to function in crisis mode when there are miscommunications or disputes related to the IEP. While educators and parents collectively want what is best for students, collaborative efforts to achieve these goals can be fragmented yielding less than optimal outcomes.

Over the last two decades, we have discovered that educator preparedness to effectively complete their jobs exists on a continuum. On one end of this continuum, educators are best prepared for practices related to the primary responsibilities of instruction. Many professionals are well trained to provide effective instruction. Their strengths reside in the ability to develop lessons that facilitate student learning. They are skilled at establishing a climate con-ducive to learning and demonstrate a strong understanding of the content to be taught.

On the other end of the continuum, educators and administrators are often ill prepared in their knowledge of the professional responsibilities that surround the work they do. They struggle with knowing the policies, procedures, and regulations that are mandated for special education services. If educators and administrators do not possess the background knowledge to adhere to the legal mandates surrounding special education, they place the school district at risk for liability issues and due process complaints. Besides being an extremely expensive venture, these disputes rarely lead to positive outcomes. The amount of energy and stress created during times of conflict between parents and school districts has a negative impact on educator morale, professional performance, and student learning.

How do educators gain the knowledge they need to perform the professional responsibilities of process, paperwork, and compliance? In effective organizational structures, educators would receive support and mentorship from administration to assist them with professional growth in all areas. What we have heard from professionals throughout the country, is that administrators often lack the training themselves. This forces administrators to take a more **evaluative role** than a **supervisory-mentor role**. The distinction here is imperative as it relates to the support and professional growth of educators. The *evaluator* rates and judges an educator's performance without providing functional feedback. This is usually completed during observations or in the end of the year summative educator evaluations. The *supervisor-mentor* observes, guides, and assists the educator in all areas of professional growth related to their duties throughout the school year. Clearly, any breakdown in leadership support can lead to ineffective organizational outcomes. It is important that educators AND administrators become knowledgeable in the legal mandates surrounding our practices as special educators (UNESCO, 2007).

This book is the overview guide introducing the S.M.A.R.T.E.R. process of goal development. This professional development is designed to provide high quality training for educators in order to improve outcomes for students in special education.

Introduction

Why should professionals and parents learn the S.M.A.R.T.E.R. STEPS™ process to develop legally compliant Individualized Education Program (IEP) goals? To fully answer this question, it is essential for us to provide some background information. There are 13 federal mandates governing IEP goals, full of jargon and confusion. In a survey of 85 special educators, 88% stated they were not adequately trained on these mandates (Ott & Wakefield, 2015).

All of the states' departments of education (DOE) were mandated to develop model IEP forms to include the federal requirements. Many professionals use their state's forms assuming that these documents meet the necessary compliance standards. Upon reviewing several state forms in our research, however, we discovered that they are missing prompts for some of the mandates (Ott & Wakefield, 2014). Educators believe they are legally secure using the IEP forms that are provided to them by their districts or states. Unfortunately, these forms may be missing federal compliance mandates that can create problems for professionals, parents, and students. The S.M.A.R.T.E.R. STEPS™ process was created to address these problems in order to provide optimal outcomes for our nation's children with special needs.

Our research revealed that there is a significant amount of stress associated with the process of developing IEP goals (Wakefield, 2004). IEP team members reported not having enough time to juggle caseloads and paperwork. They reported not having time to adequately research or remain current on evidence-based practices. Most importantly, professionals reported being unaware of the mandates that surrounded the work they do. Many educators may not have other professionals in their building for consultation about these matters. Others voiced concerns over seeing cookie cutter goals for all students, regardless of unique learning needs.

S.M.A.R.T.E.R. STEPS™ is for all members of the IEP team. When professionals and parents follow a compliant format for developing IEP goals, true collaboration can occur and IEPs can meet 100% compliance. We have trained over 5,000 school staff members and 600 families on the S.M.A.R.T.E.R. STEPS™ system to help teams understand that the purpose of the mandates is to serve students successfully.

Individualized Goal Development

First, we will tackle the idea of "What is an IEP?"

Incredibly Enormous Paperwork

We have joked that IEP stands for *Incredibly Enormous Paperwork*. Many of you may agree with this definition. IEP is supposed to represent ***Individualized Education Program***. People often think that the **P** in IEP stands for Plan, but it does not. The legal definition is program. A plan means a general outline with activities that are sketched out in various details. It tends to answer the question, "What will we do?" There is definitely a certain amount of planning needed to work with a student with special needs. In contrast, a program refers to a schedule and it is time-bound with specifics related to measurable outcomes. It answers the question, "What will be the results?" As you read further in this book, you will see why the results have become significantly more important.

An IEP document is created for children with disabilities to maximize their learning through a team effort. This document serves as the official and legal program to meet the unique learning needs of a student with a disability.

At a minimum, this program should be reviewed and updated annually to reflect the ongoing learning needs of the student. The IEP document should be designed to help teachers and related service providers understand the student's disability and how that disability impacts his or her learning. It is equally as important to have a comprehensive overview of the student's abilities and strengths when developing the IEP.

There are many important aspects to developing the IEP, but for now we will focus specifically on the definition of **individualized** as it relates to goal development.

When we discuss the concept of Individualized, goals should be:

1. Customized, rather than a cookie cutter approach
2. Updated and changed from year to year due to a child's progress
3. Driven by data based on that individual child's progress

One

Remember, without specific steps, you do not have a goal; you have wishful thinking. Unfortunately, wishful thinking will not result in progress. When there is a lack of progress, it creates stress for IEP teams because it is an indication that the program is not working. School professionals and parents are stressed out from IEPs. The most stressful part of the IEP is goal development (Wakefield, 2007).

IEPs are STRESSFUL

Why is everyone stressed from IEPs? There are nine concepts that can help us understand stressors related to developing federally compliant IEP Goals:

1. Understanding the History of IDEA
2. Time
3. Miscommunications
4. Extra Duties

1

5. FAPE and Misappropriations
6. Accountability
7. Emotional Capital
8. Financial Loss
9. Lack of Training on the 13 Federal Mandates of IEP Goals

History

First, we can increase understanding of the Individuals with Disabilities Education Act (IDEA, 1990, 1997, 2004) in general, by briefly reviewing the history of its development. Learning about the driving force, the people behind the movement, and the timeline of development can give us insight about the regulations we have in front of us today.

An original guiding principle in the education of students with disabilities was Wolfensberger's (1972) concept of normalization (Fisher, Frey, & Thousand, 2003). The normalization movement was sparked initially by the passage of the Elementary and Secondary Education Act (public law 89-10) in 1965. This law placed the responsibility of educating students with disabilities upon the public schools. As the normalization movement progressed, deinstitutionalization occurred and many students with disabilities began accessing public education in their neighborhood schools. The concept of normalization heavily influenced later legislation related to children with disabilities. Eventually, the Education for All Handicapped Children Act (EHA) was passed (public law 94-142) in 1975. This legislation put forth the notion that children with disabilities should have a right to a free and appropriate public education (FAPE).

One of the founders of IDEA was a mother from the state of Washington named Katie Dolan. She had a son with autism in the 1950s and worked with three other women to draft the first laws of special education. This law was first passed in the state of Washington in 1971 and then eventually passed as federal legislation a year later as the IDEA. The IDEA did not reach full implementation in the U.S. until 1977. This law is still young in the big picture of our nation's history on civil rights.

Once the funding and legislation were passed, there were not many guidelines to regulate the IDEA. For example, the states did not have a formal IEP process developed. Parents started making requests and suggestions. They began writing down their ideas and gave these to the school. They made requests such as:

1. "My child will feel happy at school."
2. "My son will learn to read."
3. "My daughter needs to learn about safety."

These requests were not official IEP goals though. Can you imagine serving students without IEP goals? Although it may save some time on the paperwork, it would not be in the best interest of students.

What if there were NO IEP goals?

We have to keep in mind that the special education timeline was not chronologically sequential. The law mandating special education happened before there were certified teachers in special education. Also, related services providers were not working in public schools serving children with special needs at that time. They were working in other capacities such as separate education private facilities or hospitals but not in regular education settings. Although there were speech correctionists in the public schools, they only worked with general education populations in the classroom and had caseloads from 90-500 (Whitmire, 2002).

Another important idea to remember in the timeline, universities had not yet created Bachelor's and Master's degree programs for special educators. The law was implemented before there were trained and certified staff to provide services. Fortunately, several parent groups had started working with universities on developing special education courses in the 1950s. These parent groups lobbied for passages of laws that provided funding for training of teachers who worked with children who were deaf and cognitively delayed. As a result, universities developed programs to help professionals serve children with these designated special needs (OSERS, 1997).

The University of Illinois was the first college to develop the research and training for educators and psychologists to study the non-typical development in special populations. It is important to remember that without the parents lobbying for funding of these programs in the 1950s, there would have been longer delays implementing IDEA in the public schools (OSERS, 1997).

Parents of children with special needs have historically driven the special education process (OSERS, 1997). They are the taxpayers and the stakeholders for their child's future. They are the strongest advocates for children with special needs. It is important to keep this in the forefront of your mind, because as of the 2015-2016 school year, states started surveying parents on the satisfaction of their child's IEPs. We encourage you to think about how this parental input will impact special education nationally and locally. We will discuss how parent satisfaction will be measured and how it will affect our goal development in chapter two on results-driven accountability.

Time

We have to accept that the IEP process takes time. As much as we would like to streamline the process, it would not be individualized if we copied and pasted the same goal for every student. Best practices allow IEP teams to block adequate time in their schedules for collaborative goal development and progress monitoring. Not having adequate data tracking and progress monitoring time is one of the major stressors for special education professionals.

Miscommunications

Through our practices and research, S.M.A.R.T.E.R. STEPS™ has discovered that the main area of miscommunication is due to a poorly developed IEP goal. Disputes often begin because the team rushed through the goal development process or did not collaboratively build the IEP goals. Disputes arising from these errors often cost the school district a significant amount of time and money to correct the situation. We believe that if professionals could improve this one part of the IEP, it would significantly improve parent-school relationships. In turn, fewer miscommunications and disputes would arise.

In 1986, the Regular Education Initiative (REI) was developed to address the growing concerns about the dichotomous system that had emerged in which special education and related services were viewed as separate from regular education (Will, 1986). The idea that there was not a shared responsibility or vision between both camps for children with special needs was seen as a significant problem. The REI asserted that there should be a more unified system of education instead of two separate systems. This is why collaborative IEP development and implementation between special educators and regular educators is essential to insure optimal outcomes. Otherwise, a fragmented system exists and provides a disservice to students with disabilities.

Context-focused IEP teams have advocated for a paradigm shift away from the traditional model where the classroom context is ignored (Idol, 1997; Nelson, 1994; Wallach & Butler, 1994). This non-traditional model centers on collaborative approaches in which each team member is considered an equal partner in sharing the responsibility for the students' challenges and successes. As equal partners, the team addresses the student's needs in order to determine what contexts facilitate learning. Each partner assumes roles and responsibilities related to their interests, expertise, and experience, including the parents. This begins with collaborative development of the IEP goal and progresses through to the implementation of the intervention methods.

Collaboration has been described by Idol, Nevin, and Paolucci-Whitcomb (2000) as "an interactive process that enables groups of people with diverse expertise to generate creative solutions to mutually defined problems" (p.1). The collaboration model in the context of this book is distinctly separate from that of the consultative model. The consultative model is defined as an extension of the expert model where the consultant tells other professionals what needs to be done and provides suggestions and supports to the process (Idol, Nevin, & Paolucci-Whitcomb, 2000). Conversely, collaboration is an interactive process where each team members' opinions are shared and valued equally.

Extra Duties

We understand the distractions of the job that pull special educators and related service providers away from the focus on developing and monitoring IEP goals. This is another major stressor for special education staff. We have been in your shoes and know the barriers you face with time and management of large caseloads. Some educators are expected to fulfill extra duties that can detract from IEP goal development. Every second spent on bus duty, lunch duty, or in a committee meeting is time away from serving your students. Unfortunately, the documentation requirements and legal mandates do not disappear when we are assigned extra duties.

Extra duty requirements for special educators and related services providers should be one of those issues to discuss with your supervisors. It is imperative that you engage in meaningful discussions with administration about the negative impact extra duties can have on your students' progress towards meeting IEP goals. Non-special education duties can significantly detract from the IEP goal monitoring and development.

Understanding FAPE and Misappropriations

It is important to understand the following two terms: misappropriations and free appropriate public education (FAPE). Misappropriation refers to funds that are specifically earmarked for certain students or programs but are not spent on them. FAPE refers to providing appropriate specialized education programs for students and they demonstrate educational benefit as a result of it. FAPE is a federal mandate (IDEA, 2004).

In reviewing misappropriations, imagine if funds were donated to the school specifically for a grass field for the football stadium. Instead of spending that money on the stadium, the school bought computers with it. That would be a misappropriation of funds.

If the federal and state governments provide local districts with funds for special education salaries, then that money needs to be concentrated on special education students. If special education teachers spend an hour of their week at bus duty for regular education students, then that results in 36-40 hours taken away from special education students by the end of the school year. That would be a misappropriation of funds.

If the school district is audited for that type of pattern what do you think could happen? What do you think would happen if one of the students on your caseload did not make progress toward their IEP goals if you spent 60 minutes a week on bus duty for all students instead of planning or progress monitoring? It may be considered that you were not providing a free appropriate public education (FAPE) to the students with special needs. If students are not meeting all of their IEP goals, then the district is in jeopardy of not meeting FAPE for that student.

Accountability

In the past, a district may not have been scrutinized if their students were not meeting IEP goals. As of the 2015-2016 school year, however, accountability measures on IEP goal progress by the state and federal departments of education will matter. Can you see why it is crucial that the focus of your day should be guided by IEP goals? Time spent on other types of non-learning tasks at your job should be significantly minimized unless you can justify that those duties advance a student on his or her IEP goals. You can help administrators understand that the IDEA law stipulates that funding for your position is designated specifically for the purpose of helping students meet IEP goals. Special education contracts should be updated to reflect only those duties related to serving the needs of special education students.

Emotional Capital

Emotional capital refers to the feelings, beliefs, and energy that an IEP team invests in a student. If teams invest a significant amount of emotional capital into a student, they expect a positive, successful outcome for that student. This provides a rewarding and fulfilling experience to educators because they create the learning environment to assist the student with achieving his or her future endeavors. This is truly the main reason why educators invest so much of their energy into children. What happens to emotional capital when there is a dispute? What happens to the fulfilling feelings? What happens to the energy?

Professionals involved in special education disputes are profoundly affected by these events. When asked to characterize the degree of stress experienced during a due process hearing or subsequent litigation, research by the American Association of School Administrators (AASA) indicated that 95% of respondents classified the stress as high or very high (Pudelski, 2016). Twelve percent of school administrators said that over 50% of district special education personnel either left the district or requested a transfer out of special education after being involved in due process procedures.

Further, the research indicated that although a significant amount of emotional capital was invested in the due process, there was minimal connection to improving the educational outcomes of the student involved (Pudelski, 2016). AASA asserts that schools need to rethink how parents and districts resolve disputes. One important idea is to engage in prevention strategies in goal development so that these problems do not occur in the first place.

Financial Loss

According to AASA's executive summary (April, 2016), the average legal fees for a district involved in a due process hearing were $10,512.50. When districts were ordered to compensate parents for their attorney's fees, the average expenditure increased to $19,241.38. The costs associated with the verdict of the due process hearing averaged districts $15,924.14. For districts that chose to settle with a parent prior to the due process hearing, the settlement costs averaged $23,827.34.

After all of this money has been spent, there is no evidence demonstrating that successful challenges to an IEP in a due process hearing lead to improvements in education for students with disabilities (Pudelski, 2016). This is a significant concern for the procedural safeguards of students with IEPs in our nation. No research proves that students who take advantage of IDEA's due process provisions fare better academically after undertaking mediation, child complaint, or due process. Clearly, there needs to be a better way to address these problems.

Lack of Training on the 13 Federal Mandates

In 2015, our survey research indicated that 88% of school staff lacked training in IEP goal mandates. When educators are not provided with adequate training on the legal requirements, it can create stress, disputes, and official complaints. The survey conclusions indicate that there needs to be some type of training process to assist professionals with understanding the mandates. After reviewing the mandates, we realized why they were so challenging to incorporate into IEP goals. These mandates are full of jargon, fragmented, and difficult to remember. We recognized that there needs to be a user-friendly way to recall all the requirements. This resulted in the development of an acronym as a memory device. The 13 federal mandates fit into the acronym S.M.A.R.T.E.R. as an easy prompting system for IEP teams. Goals should be:

Specific
Measurable
Attainable and accountable
Research and evidence-based
Teachable
Evaluated and communicated
Relevant to general/alternative curriculum

The S.M.A.R.T.E.R. acronym will be reviewed in-depth in Chapter Four. The accountability movement was sparked in 2001 with the reauthorization of the Elementary and Secondary Education Act, also known as No Child Left Behind (PL 107-110). This has affected special education with mandates from the U.S. Department of Education Office of Special Education (OSERS) for districts to engage in results driven accountability.

TWO

RESULTS DRIVEN ACCOUNTABILITY (RDA)

Accountability for IEP goal progress has emerged as the main defining factor for demonstrating FAPE. In the 2015-2016 school year, there were changes in government and state progress monitoring for special education services. Each state's department of education (DOE) started scrutinizing student level results for the following populations with IEPs:

- preschool
- alternative assessment students
- transition age and older
- high school graduates

For all populations, the states reviewed "state-identified measurable results" which were described as "a child-level outcome and not a process-level outcome", (RDA Summary, 2014). OSERS used test scores of IEP students as one of their main outcome indicators for accountability.

There have been numerous paradigm shifts in the past 40 years in special education. More than ever, districts will need to improve their skills with developing attainable IEP goals. This shift is a framework called Results-Driven Accountability (RDA).

The federal government provides 40% of the funding for special education programs and this funding may become conditional in the future (RDA Summary, 2014). In 2012-2013, OSERS decided to restructure how they monitored the states' special education programs. They developed a rubric to grade states that was significantly different than what they had ever implemented previously. This RDA rubric is planned out for five years and schools are expected to meet high percentages of their targets in these five years. The 2012-2013 school year was the baseline year.

OSERS wanted to track the states' progress on certain student outcomes. OSERS found that only 15 states (shown in green) met the federal criteria. The thirty-five states in yellow were considered *needs improvement* and funding could become conditional. Four states including California, Texas, Delaware, and Washington DC required intervention and were at-risk for losing federal funding. Take a moment and find your state on the map.

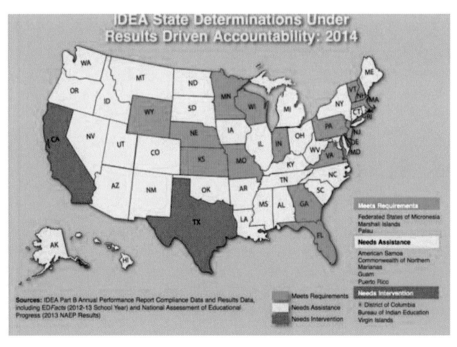

IDEA Part B Annual Performance Report Compliance
Data and Result Data (RDA Summary, 2014)

What do these categories mean? According to OSERS, if a state needs assistance for two years in a row, IDEA requires the United States Department of Education (U.S. DOE) to take action against the state. For example, the U.S. DOE will require the states to obtain technical assistance or identify the state as a high-risk grant recipient. Should a state need intervention for three years in a row, IDEA mandates that the state's DOE must take specific actions, such as:

1. prepare a corrective action plan
2. enter into a compliance agreement
3. limit state's funding

The second map shows the 2013-2014 school year data. You can see that some of the states changed to green or yellow. This may appear that there was improvement. We suggest you interpret this with caution related to how the measures were obtained. In the baseline year (2012-2013) and follow-up year (2013-2014), the states' DOEs were allowed to choose the districts they wanted for reporting data to OSERS. As of the 2015-16 school year, the states' DOEs will be mandated to report on *all* of the districts in the state for all four of the population indicators of the RDA. The point of this requirement is to reduce the biased sampling. It is important to be careful in recognizing that just because your state is green one year, it does not mean your state will be green the following year.

STATE SPECIAL EDUCATION RATINGS

In June 2015, the U.S. Department of Education released its most recent evaluation of how well states are meeting the requirements of the Individuals with Disabilities Eduction Act, covering the 2013-14 school year. No state received the lowest ranking, needs substantial intervention. However, several states fell into the needs assistance or needs intervention categories for two or more years, which triggers certain enforcement actions from the department.

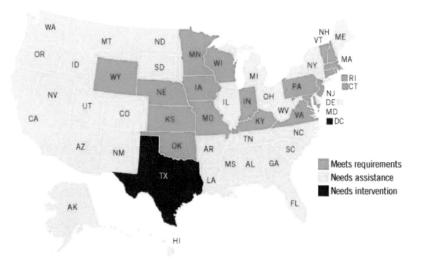

SOURCE: U.S. Department of Education, office of special education programs

EDUCATION WEEK

IDEA Part B Annual Performance Summary Compliance Data and Results Data (Samuels, Education Week, July 6, 2015).

With RDA, OSERS has funded a $50 million technical assistance center called the Center on Systemic Improvement. It will help states leverage the $11.5 billion in federal special education funds that they currently receive to improve outcomes for students with disabilities. In addition, OSERS will be working with each state to support them in developing comprehensive plans designed to improve results for children with disabilities. The focus of RDA is an emphasis on documenting the evidence-based strategies that are being used to achieve student outcomes.

What if there were NO IEP goals?

Baseline Data: Due February 1, 2015, *the state must provide 2013 baseline data expressed as a percentage* and is aligned with the State-Identified Measurable Results for Children with Disabilities.

Targets: Due February 1, 2015, *the State must provide measurable and rigorous targets (expressed as percentages) for each of the five years from FFY 2014 through FFY 2018.* The State's FFY 2018 target must demonstrate improvement over the State's FFY 2013 baseline data.

Updated Data: In its FFYs 2014 through 2018, due February 2016 through February 2020, *the State must provide updated data for that specific FFY (expressed as a percentage) and that data must be aligned with the State-identified Measurable Results for Children with Disabilities.* The State must report on whether it met its target.

In reviewing the RDA's target populations for monitoring, one of the focus areas of importance will be the preschool population. They are reviewing data on children with IEPs to determine the percentage of IEP students who have met their goals. The areas of pragmatic language, communication skills, early literacy skills, and behavior skills will be studied. The RDA grading rubric is detailed and lengthy. Below is an example of the language in the requirements.

Percent of Children Aged 3 through 5 who demonstrate improved:

1. Positive social-emotional skills (including social relationships)
2. Acquisition and use of knowledge and skills (early language, communication and early literacy; and
3. Use of appropriate behaviors to meet their needs.

(20 U.S.C. 1416 (a)(3)(A))

There are measurement formulas for all of the items on this rubric. The preschool population has their own sub-section and site on systemic improvement called the Early Education Center. If you have not checked out this site, we highly recommend that you spend some time reviewing it. The site has many valuable resources for you (https://www.wested.org/project/national-center-for-systemic-improvement/).

The next population under review will be students who turn 16 during the IEP (Transition Age). The RDA will focus on the IEP goals related to transition, post-secondary, and independent living.

Percent of youth aged 16 and above with IEPs that include

1. Appropriate measurable postsecondary goals that are annually updated and based upon an age appropriate transition assessment
2. Transition services, including courses of study that will reasonably enable the student to meet those postsecondary goals
3. Annual IEP goals related to the student's transition service needs
4. Evidence that the student was invited to the IEP meeting
5. Evidence that a representation from participating transition agencies was invited with prior consent of the parent or student

(20 U.S.C. 1416 (a)(3)(A))

In addition to preschool and transition age populations, OSERS will be reviewing how all students with IEPs perform on state mandated testing. Of course, some states do not test every grade level. In those cases, states may review IEP goal outcomes for the untested grades. Alternative assessment students will be reviewed on their goal progress as well.

Participation and performance of children on IEPs on statewide assessments

A. Percent of districts with a disability subgroup that meets the state's AYP targets
B. Participation rates for children with IEPs
C. Proficiency rate for children with IEPs against grade level, modified, and alternative academic achievement standards
(20 U.S.C. 1416 (a)(3)(A))

The U.S. DOE is now requiring states to use a child-level outcome instead of a process outcome. Process outcomes from the past were indicators such as:

1. Did schools complete evaluations within 60 days?
2. Did schools send out child find notices?
3. How many Notices of Action were completed?
4. How many mediation meetings did states conduct?

The state DOEs were never measuring the direct outcomes of students in the past. Why would there be a shift from process to student outcomes? OSERS focused on process for nine years, so why would they care about actual results of students? That may sound like an unnecessary question, but it is an important part of understanding this shift. The four main reasons for this shift include:

a. Parent concerns and advocacy
b. Low NAEP scores for reading and math of IEP students
c. Low alternative assessment outcomes for IEP students
d. Low graduation rates of IEP students

Another critical part of this RDA rubric is that parents will be reporting if schools facilitated parent involvement. Furthermore, parents will be surveyed to determine if parent involvement improved their child's performance as a result. This must be completed through surveys or letters directly from the parents. It cannot be measured as a process such as percentage of parental attendance at IEP meetings. This is a major change for many states. You may want to investigate how your district intends to implement this regulation. If your school has not started measuring parent engagement, then you should probably inform your administrators that it is a significant factor in the rubric.

It seems obvious why parents would want results. Of course, they want their children to be as successful as possible, similar to parents of non-disabled children. Unfortunately, there has not been adequate accountability on this issue. One of the main accountability complaints by parents to the DOE centers on the fact that children are not meeting IEP goals. For example, the Missouri DOE created an annual review of the top ten reasons for parent disputes (MO DESE, 2015). Problems with IEP Goals were listed as the third main reason for child complaints and due process.

A recent landmark case in Roseland, New Jersey highlighted this situation and sets precedence (Sussan, Greenwald, & Wesler, 2015). On July 27, 2015, in T.O. et al v. Summit City Board of Education, the United States District Court affirmed the July 2, 2012 decision of an Administrative Law Judge (ALJ). The ALJ maintained that Summit Schools failed to provide FAPE to a student, J.O. The Court noted that J.O.'s parents had attempted to work cooperatively with Summit School District for a year. The Court cited the ALJ's finding that "Summit responded to the parents' and private therapists' suggestions only with token gestures intended to placate them." Further, the Court stated that IEPs must be specific. The Court highlighted the importance of goals that are reasonable and achievable. The Court upheld the ALJ's conclusion that the Summit District's IEP was not tailored for J.O.'s disability. It included some goals that were unattainable given his disability and other goals that were set too low. In sum, the Court disapproved of the school's use of cookie cutter goals and blocking meaningful parent involvement. The district was found out of compliance. Appeals may continue for this case as parents seek reimbursement for compensatory services.

Working with parents can be a challenge on many levels. We have seen the continuum with regard to home-school relationships. Some educators are engaged in situations where parents have limited involvement in the IEP. Other professionals have the opposite issue with highly involved parents. These parents are frequently calling, emailing and wanting answers to difficult questions. Regardless of the challenge, we must learn to develop ways to manage the parent involvement and input because it will play a major role in future accountability measures.

At S.M.A.R.T.E.R. STEPS™, we have attended over 2,000 IEP meetings in 20 years across five different states. Through our work, we have discovered that most IEP teams do not know how to develop goals according to federal guidelines. Children may be making progress, but it is difficult to tell because of how the goals have been developed and monitored. Several factors come into play here:

1. Goals are not specific enough to be measured adequately.
2. Measurement procedures are not clearly defined.
3. Measurement procedures do not match the target skill set.

Sometimes, professionals have unknowingly created impossible situations for themselves and for their students. In review of our own practices, we had no idea that there were 13 specific considerations that were legally required for an IEP goal. Countless hours have been spent in district in-services, yet this information about the mandates for IEP Goals was never distributed. We surveyed special educators in 2015 and discovered that 88% had not been trained on these 13 mandates. If educators lack training on how to develop IEP goals, it is easy to understand why they experience stress. How can we educate ourselves?

Three

13 Federal Mandates

The following is a review of the 13 Federal Mandates related to IEP Goals. Each mandate includes the legal excerpt first, then a summary of the excerpt's meaning.

Requirement 1: Specific areas of need
Present Level of Academic and Functional Progress

- (A) In general, in developing each child's IEP, the IEP Team, subject to subparagraph (C), shall consider [34 CFR §300.320(2),1(a)]
- (iv) the academic, developmental, and functional needs of the child. [34 CFR §300.320(2),1(a)]

The first requirement is the specific areas of need for a student. This is supposed to include academic, developmental, and functional needs of the child. Be careful to avoid saying, "We only have to look at academics or grades" because that would be omitting the developmental *and* functional mandates of IDEA. Examples of developmental and functional areas can include but are not limited to: social skills, behavior regulation, executive functioning, executive functioning, and safety issues.

Requirements 2 and 3: Other educational needs, measurable, relevant to general education curriculum, progress monitoring, contexts.
A statement of **measurable** annual goals, including academic and functional goals designed to:

- Meet the child's needs that result from the child's disability to enable the child to be involved in and make progress in the general education curriculum. [34 CFR §300.320(a)(2)(i)(A)]
- Meet each of the child's other educational needs that result from the child's disability. [34 CFR §300.320(a)(2)(i)(B)].

The second and third requirements refer to any other educational needs that result from the disability. This is where all the related services are referenced. Also, we have the concept of measurability playing into the equation now. This is the first mention of relevancy of the goal to the general education curriculum.

Requirement 4: Specific needs expanded to include benchmarks for alternative assessments

- For children with disabilities who take alternative assessments aligned to alternate achievement standards (in addition to the annual goals), a description of benchmarks or short-term objectives. [34 CFR §300.320(a)(2)(ii)]

The specific needs are expanded further to include alternative assessments with benchmarks and short-term objectives. Benchmarks are the incremental objectives that must be attained in order for the annual goal to be met. For example, a student may need to show mastery of short-term goals of sight words in isolation before progressing to reading them in simple sentences for the annual goal.

Requirement 5: Measurable, data collection, frequency, baselines, and what is considered mastery

A description of:

- How the Child's progress toward meeting the annual goals will be measured [34 CFR §300.320(a)(3)(i)]

This mandate refers to your evaluation system and the data that you will be gathering. This is important because teams often forget baselines, data collection frequency, and criteria for mastery.

Requirement 6: Evaluation of the data and communication to parents

- Designate when periodic reports on the progress the child is making toward meeting the annual goals will be provided such as through the use of quarterly or other periodic reports, and at least as frequent as concurrent with the issuance of report cards. [34 CFR §300.320(a)(3)(ii)]

The sixth requirement involves periodic evaluations of the data. The data must be reported at certain intervals determined by the team but at least as often as report cards. The periodic progress evaluations in this section refer to reports that are communicated to parents.

Requirements 7, 8, and 9: Research-based services, teachable cues, strategies, and supplementary aids

- A statement of the special education and related services and supplemental aids and services, based on peer-reviewed research to the extent practicable, to be provided to the child, or on behalf of the child, and a statement of the program modifications or supports for school personnel that will be provided to enable the child [34 CFR 300.320 (a)(4)

Requirements seven, eight, and nine relate to research and evidence-based requirements for special education, related services, and supplementary aids being used to attain progress. We suggest that there must be a documented statement somewhere about the research or evidence-based teaching methods and strategies. If not documentend in the IEP, the evidence base related to the service or supplementary aid needs to be noted in the child's file or in progress notes. This has been a requirement since 2004, although rarely do school districts document this as mandated. In addition, the evidence base must relate to the skill sets and behaviors that are teachable with cues and strategies.

Requirements 10, 11, and 12: Attainable, relevant to general education curriculum, and participation with non-disabled peers

- To advance appropriately toward attaining the annual goals [34 CFR §300.320(a)(4)(i)]
- To be involved in and make progress in the general education curriculum and to participate in extracurricular and other nonacademic activities [34 CFR §300.320(a)(4)(ii)]
- To be educated and participate with other children with disabilities and nondisabled children in extracurricular and other nonacademic activities [34 CFR §300.320(a)(4)(iii)]

Requirements 10, 11, and 12 relate to a goal being attainable within an IEP cycle. Also, relevancy to the general education curriculum is mentioned again. Finally, participation with non-disabled peers is referenced. This refers to the context and ties back to the specific skill sets we mentioned earlier.

Requirement 13: Transition relevant to employment, post-secondary, or independent living

- Beginning no later than the first IEP to be in effect when the child turns 16, or younger if determined appropriate by the IEP team, and updated annually thereafter, the IEP must include:
- Appropriate measurable postsecondary goals based upon age appropriate transition assessments related to training, education, employment, and where appropriate, independent living skills [34 CFR §300.320(b)(1)]
- Transition services (including courses of study) needed to assist the child in reaching those goals [34 CFR §300.320(b)(2)]

Transition services are focusing on the same ideas that have been mentioned in the previous mandates: specific, measurable, attainable, and research-based. The relevancy part needs to be employment-related or pertaining to post-secondary education or independent living skills instead of the general education curriculum.

This is an extensive amount of information for anyone to remember. This is the reason why it is challenging to incorporate all of these mandates into IEP goals. The S.M.A.R.T.E.R. method was developed to help professionals manage all of this information.

The IEP Process

| How the special education admini- strator explained it. | How the parent envisioned what the admini- strator said. | How the IEP team thought they were supposed to imple- ment it. | What the child needed. |

Four

We like the idea of working S.M.A.R.T.E.R. rather than harder. You may be familiar with SMART goals, as these have existed in other professional arenas for years. The original S.M.A.R.T. goal was developed by George T. Doran in 1981 for Fortune 500 companies. This acronym stood for specific, measurable, assignable, realistic and timely. We expanded the acronym to include all the IEP mandates for developing goals as follows:

Specific
Measurable
Attainable and accountable
Research and evidence-based
Teachable
Evaluated and communicated
Relevant to general/alternative curriculum

Specific

A specific goal has a greater chance of being accomplished than a general goal. To set a specific goal, you must answer the six "Wh" questions:

1. Who: Who is involved?
2. What: What do I want to accomplish?
3. Where: Where will I accomplish it?
4. When: When will I accomplish it?
5. Which: Which requirements and constraints will be in place?
6. Why: Why should I accomplish this goal?

For example, a general goal would read: "Get in shape." In contrast, a specific goal would read: "Sue will join a health club and workout 3 days a week to lose 10 pounds in 4 weeks."

Measurable

It is important to establish concrete criteria for measuring progress toward the attainment of each goal you set. When we measure progress, we tend to stay on track. We reach target dates and gain motivation to continue efforts toward goals. To determine if your goal is measurable, ask questions such as "How much?" or "How many?" Next, ask yourself, "How will I know when it is accomplished?" You should be thinking about the end product. Ask yourself, "What should this look like when it is achieved?"

A goal that merely states: "Child will demonstrate age appropriate vocabulary," would be difficult to progress monitor. How can you make that goal more specific? You can designate specific vocabulary and level expectations such as: "Child will demonstrate understanding of grade 3 science vocabulary related to classroom learning with 80% accuracy for 5 consecutive units." Remember, it has to be a behavior that you can see and count. That is an easy way to explain it to parents and teachers. Can we see it? How can we count it?

Teams should avoid using non-specific verbs that are difficult to visualize and count such as:

1. Student will **improve**
2. Student will **increase**

3. Student will **decrease**
4. Student will **be appropriate**
5. Student will **demonstrate**

Goals should contain action words such as:

answer	express	summarize	ambulate
apply	grasp	phonate	ascend
categorize	label	touch	descend
choose	match	self-correct	self-propel
imitate	predict	generalize	dictate
identify	produce	alternate	restate
fasten	recite	select	differentiate

Sometimes, IEP teams set up situations that are too difficult to track with the system they have devised. Avoid being stuck in a measuring trap that is unrealistic for you or the teachers. Sometimes, even though it looked good on paper, it may not be practical for daily monitoring.

Another barrier we have identified results when we get stuck in the "percentages trap". Besides percentages, there are other ways to measure progress that may be more appropriate to the situation. Here are some options to consider:

1. Likert Scales
2. Rubrics
3. Repetitions to mastery
4. Duration in time (stamina in minutes)
5. Length across an area (steps, feet)
6. Portfolio items
7. Strategy Log
8. Items entered for mastery (number of books read)
9. Contract completion

Attainable

When you identify goals that are most important for the student's progress, you begin to figure out ways to make them come true. Most goals can be attained when you plan your steps wisely and establish a time frame that allows you to progress. There are several questions to consider when determining if a goal is attainable:

1. Has the student accomplished something similar in the past?
2. Does the student have absences or illnesses that could interfere?
3. Is there a history of regression? What is the severity of the student's disability?
4. What is the total amount of intervention that student is receiving for the school year?

For example, a standard amount of speech therapy is one hour per week. What can realistically be accomplished in 36 hours of intervention in school year? What increment of progress will occur in those total hours? Imagine that you had previous data for a student that showed he could gain a 20% increase in accuracy on a discrete articulation skill after 20 hours of intervention. If that same student had a baseline of 40% on a new articulation goal, is 90% mastery criterion an attainable level within a school year? Most likely, this would not be an appropriate goal for this student. Each goal should be grounded within a time frame. Remaining cognizant of that time frame helps teams feel the urgency to keep data and analyze progress. Ask yourself what conditions must exist for the student to accomplish this goal.

Research-Based

The Elementary and Secondary Education Act (ESEA, 2001) and the Reauthorization of IDEA (2006) mandated that schools use evidence-based methods. This means teams need to use current peer-reviewed practices to provide high quality services. (Yell & Rosalski, 2013).

There have been three litigation cases that have directly addressed the peer-reviewed research mandate.

1. Waukee Community School District (2007)
2. Rocklin Unified School District (2007)
3. Ridley School District (2012)

In the Waukee case, the administrative law judge (ALJ) ruled that the procedures used by the student's teacher were (a) not implemented in a manner consistent with peer-reviewed research or appropriate educational practices, (b) not adequately monitored, and (c) not consistent with IDEA's positive behavior supports mandate. The district was found in violation of FAPE.

The Rocklin case had a different outcome. The ALJ ruled in favor of the school district because they had documentation of an eclectic program they used. The ALJ stated that the district did not have to use the greatest body of peer-reviewed research for their methods. The program and evidence base that the district used was considered reasonable enough to provide educational benefit. Note that the district had an evidence base documented to support them in this case.

The Ridley case is more complicated and has various facets to it. The focus for the purpose of this discussion is that the hearing officer found that the proposed IEP was inadequate. The hearing officer stated that the IEP lacked specially designed instruction in the form of a research-based, peer-reviewed reading program. The hearing officer awarded the parents compensatory education and reimbursement for tuition at a private school.

Federal and state laws regulate that we use research-based practices to ensure that our services are efficient and effectively delivered. This is one of the most challenging aspects for professionals. We need to learn how to review the evidence and apply it. There are some great resources available to help such as: ERIC, Cochrane Library, PubMed, Google Scholar, and our professional organization's research portals.

Teachable

It is important to document what strategies, prompts, or cues you will be using in your goal. It helps any other professional involved with that student know instructional methods to implement. One word of caution here: It is never a good idea to name specific programs, therapy materials, or other expensive items in your goals. In doing so, the district becomes responsible for purchasing and providing those resources. For example, you would not say, "using the Wilson's Reading Program". Instead, you could say, "using a structured phonological coding system."

Evaluated and Communicated to Parents

Remember, it is extremely important to keep accurate data in order to effectively track, assess, and report progress to parents. We are accountable for the services we provide and need to keep some form of data. While some school staff record daily logs, others do a weekly progress check. How do you communicate progress to parents? While working in schools, we often heard complaints from staff about not having time to maintain routine communication with parents. We heard complaints from parents that they did not like a certain style of communication such as email, or they had specific preferences. We all know the challenges we face when trying to accommodate multiple preferences. Do you use a cookie cutter approach (i.e., Friday folders for all) or do you accommodate individual preferences? Some schools have switched to an online tracking tool where parents have access daily to their child's progress. The advantage of this system allows you to enter data, and it places the responsibility of checking progress on the parent so there can be teamwork in accountability.

Relevant

Federal mandates require goals to support and allow access to the general education curriculum that is reflected by dovetailing with state standards.

Aligning goals to state standards can be a challenge for specific, discrete, lower developmental skills. This is why it is important to adjust this mandate to include your state's alternative curriculum. Also, for students who are 16 years of age or older, the goal needs to be relevant to post-secondary, transition, and independent living goals.

As school staff, we know that a child needs to attain specific hierarchical benchmarks toward larger objectives and even more general goals. It is important to remember, that while we may see indirect links from goals to academic standards, it is our responsibility to make those clear and understandable to parents.

Summary of Process

1. We test and identify areas of weakness.
2. We identify and prioritize which deficits affect learning in the present level of performance.
3. We draft goals that are specific, measurable, and attainable.
4. We review specific areas of learning impacted and determine where the draft goals fit in with the curriculum (general, alternative, post-secondary, transition, or independent living skills).
5. We ensure that we completed every level of S.M.A.R.T.E.R. STEPS™.

Five

In order to better understand the S.M.A.R.T.E.R. STEPS™ process, it is helpful to review examples of S.M.A.R.T.E.R. STEPS™ goals. The first five goals will be developed for a student named Dorothy who is in the sixth grade. Then, there will be four subsequent examples with different students.

Background: Dorothy lives with her aunt and uncle in Kansas. She suffered a mild head injury in a tornado. She has a diagnosis of anxiety disorder. She struggles with some articulation issues due to dysarthria. She has language concerns in the areas of using correct word order during oral presentations. Also, she has difficulty retaining grade level vocabulary in science and social studies. This student has significantly delayed development of irregular past tense verbs. Finally, she is unaware of when she needs to take a turn in large group discussions in class.

Example Goal 1
Area of Need: Speech

Annual Goal: Dorothy will produce conversational speech with an average rating of 3 on the Likert Intelligibility Scale during language arts small group discussions as rated by the teacher for 3 out of 4 sampling days for 3 consecutive months. Data will be gathered once per week and evaluated monthly.

Teacher will be seated by the visual cue station during discussions to promote carry-over (Koegel, Koegel, & Ingham, 1986).

Scale Baselines: 2.0 (Dec. 2013) 2.5 (May, 2014)

Likert Intelligibility Scale

    1- requires frequent clarifications by teacher
    2- requires clarifications sometimes by teacher
    3- rarely requires clarifications by teacher

Progress will be communicated to parents monthly via email by SLP. SLP will email teacher weekly with Likert Scale to collect data.

Aligns with CCSS ELA Literacy SL6.4. "clear pronunciation"

———

So we ask ourselves, is it:

Specific?	Yes: Action word and context provided
Measurable?	Yes: Likert scale with baseline and criterion level
Attainable?	Yes: Baselines show progression
Research based?	Yes: Cited for cue type
Teachable?	Yes: Using a visual cue station
Evaluated and communicated?	Yes: monthly data will be emailed
Relevant to curriculum?	Yes: aligns with literacy standard

When viewing this goal in this narrative manner, it may seem overwhelming. We have entered the goal in to a Missouri model IEP form to demonstrate how it would typically look in and IEP document (MO DESE, 2016).

IEP Goal with Objectives/Benchmarks and a Reporting Form			
Area of Need: Speech			

Annual Goal #: 1: Dorothy will produce conversational speech with an average rating of 3 on the Likert Intelligibility Scale during language arts small group discussions as rated by the teacher for 3 out of 4 sampling days for 3 consecutive months. Data will be gathered once per week and evaluated monthly.

Teacher will be seated by the visual cue station during discussions to promote carry-over (Koegel, Koegel, & Ingham, 1986)

For students with Post-Secondary Transition Plans, indicate which goal domain(s) this annual goal will support:

☐ Post-secondary Education/Training   ☐ Employment   ☐ Independent Living

The Goal is relevant to:_ X General Education Curriculum
____ Alternative Curriculum

Standard: Aligns with CCSS ELA Literacy SL6.4. "clear pronunciation"

Progress toward the goal will be measured by: **(check all that apply)**

☐ Work samples	☐ Curriculum based tests	☐ Portfolios	☐ Checklists
☐ Scoring guides	☐ Observation chart	☐ Reading record	☒ Other: LIKERT SCALE

Progress Reporting: Progress will be communicated to parents monthly via email by SLP
SLP will email teacher weekly with Likert Scale to collect data.

Progress Toward the Goal

Date of Report	12/1/13	5/5/14	/ /	/ /	/ /	/ /
Making progress toward annual goal	2.0	2.5				
Not making progress toward annual goal						
Goal not addressed this reporting period						
Goal met						

Comments: Likert Intelligibility Scale
    1- requires frequent clarifications by teacher
    2- requires clarifications sometimes by teacher
    3- rarely requires clarifications by teacher

Missouri Model Form

Example Goal 2
Area of Need: Syntax

Annual Goal: Dorothy will produce sentences with correct word order during oral presentations in the classroom with 80% accuracy in language arts and social studies classes. Scripting, video-practice 1:1, and shape-coding templates will be used for cues to assist her (Ebbels, 2007).

Data will be gathered 4 times per trimester during presentations and communicated to parents with trimester report cards.

Baseline: 50% on May, 2014.

Aligns with CCSS ELA-Literacy SL 6.6 "demonstrate command of formal English"

Here is the goal on a model IEP form from Colorado:

ANNUAL GOALS (OBJECTIVES, IF REQUIRED) IDEA 300.320(a)(2)(i)	
For transition IEPs, annual goals MUST link directly to postsecondary goals.	
☐ Check here if this is an **Extended School Year Goal**	
Area of Need: Syntax	
Measurable Goal: IDEA 300.320(a)(2)(i) Dorothy will produce sentences with correct word order during oral presentations in the classroom with 80% accuracy in language arts and social studies classes. Scripting, video-practice 1:1, and shape-coding templates will be used for cues to assist her (Ebbels, 2007).	**Unit of Measurement:** IDEA 300.320(a)(3)(i)
	Percentage accuracy on word order in oral
Objective (if needed): IDEA 300.320(a)(2)(B)(ii)	**presentations**
Related Colorado Academic Standard/Extended Evidence Outcomes: ELA-Literacy SL 6.6 demonstrate command of formal English	**Baseline Data Point:** **50% 5/2/14**
Evaluation Method: ☐Monitor and Chart Progress ☐ Focused Assessments ☐ Portfolio Collection X Other:__Oral Presentation score sheets IDEA 300.320(a)(3)(i)	
Progress Report (Describe how parents will be informed of the student's progress toward goals and how frequently this will occur) IDEA 300.320(a)(3)(iii) Data will be gathered 4 times per trimester during presentations and communicated to parents with trimester report cards.	

Reporting Date: __/__/__	Reporting Date: __/__/__	Reporting Date: __/__/__	Reporting Date: __/__/__
Progress: ____ Supporting Data Point:	Progress: ____ Supporting Data Point:	Progress: ____ Supporting Data Point:	Progress: ____ Supporting Data Point:

Colorado Model form (CO DESE, 2016)

Example Goal 3
Area of Need: Semantics
Annual Goal: Dorothy will complete semantic maps for a portfolio for 10 words per week for science and 10 words per week for social studies for a total of 10 units each class (instead of quizzes).

Word counts will be completed weekly by teachers and will be emailed to parents weekly.

SLP will support linguistic underpinnings of this goal as a related service.

Teachers will select the 10 words and provide prompts for the semantic maps.

Baseline: 0 / 10 units completed

Research: Semantic maps (Heimlich & Pittleman, 1986) Linguistic Underpinnings (Ehren, 2000).

Aligns with ELA L.6.4: Determine the meaning of unknown words based on grade 6 content.

Example Goal 4
Area of Need: Morphology
Annual Goal: Dorothy will identify 30/30 of the most frequently used irregular past tense verbs during monthly English assessments in multiple choice format. Monthly scores will be emailed to parents. Distributed practice during structured journal tasks 3 times per week during English class will be provided as intervention by SLP.

Baseline: 4/30

Research: Distributed direct practice of irregular past tense (Proctor-Williams, Fey, 2007)

Aligns with ELA, Literacy W 6.4: "produce clear and coherent writing".

Example Goal 5
Area of Need: Pragmatics
Annual Goal: Dorothy will achieve an average of 3 verbal turns during a 15-minute book group discussion once per week during English class for the first trimester. Turns will be cued through the guided question worksheets and predictable turn-taking routines. Turns will be tallied on the sheet by D. to promote self-monitoring. Goal will be reviewed at trimester with parents to determine if increase in turns is needed.

Baseline: 1 turn during 15 minutes.

Teacher will consult with SLP on data tracking.
Research: Written text cues and predictable turn taking routines (Thiesman & Goldstein, 2001)

Aligns with ELA-Literacy SL6.1B: "Follow rules for collegial discussions."

Example Goal 6
Background: Evan, age 4, fronts /k/ and /g/. He has normal hearing and vision. He is unable to hear the difference between /k/ and /t/ or /g/ and /d/ in CVC minimal word pairs (can/tan or gun/done).

Area of Need: Speech (preschooler in California)
Annual Goal: Evan will identify the /k/ sound in the initial positions of CVC words with an average of 70% accuracy in structured tasks with pictures.

Modified cued speech hand signals and mirror feedback will be used for intervention (Cornett & Daisey, 1992, 2001; Chilson, 1979; Kaplan, 1974).

Minimal contrast pairs will be used as a secondary intervention (Baker, 2010; Blache, Parsons, & Humphreys, 1981; Weiner, 1981).

Selection criteria will be presented to him in a binary choice format. Data will be gathered 2 times per month.

Averages will be calculated quarterly and reported to parents via report cards.

Baseline: 40% on probe list at preschool screening (seemed to be random guessing so the accuracy of baseline needs to be taken into consideration as the task was a binary choice pointing set-up).

Aligns with general education: "Preschool Learning Frameworks".
Language Strand-Listening and Speaking: 1.0 Language Use and Conventions: "Speak Clearly".

Example Goal 7

Background: Jaden is a 6th grade student with multiple disabilities. He has severe autism. He is non-verbal but can use some gestures inconsistently. Also, he can use a communication device with a few picture cues. The main concern is that he needs to locate and access his device when prompted. Jaden has arm restraints for self-harm. This is one of the limitations for him in learning more sophisticated signing systems.

Area of Need: Communication (Alternative Curriculum/Benchmarks)
   Annual Goal: Jaden will engage in communication exchanges in structured tasks by achieving 3/3 benchmarks below:

Benchmarks

1. Jaden will **locate** device for an average of 60% of opportunities across 3 of 5 data collection days per month by locating it with faded visual cues (West, 2008).

    Baseline is 0% of opportunities. Qualitative cue data: Requires __ reminders

2. Jaden will **access** his device for an average of 60% of opportunities across 3 of 5 data collection days per month by locating it with faded visual cues (West, 2008).

    Baseline is 0% of opportunities. Qualitative cue data: Requires __ reminders

3. Jaden will demonstrate 4/4 following gestures to communicate independently in structured settings (Daniels, 1996; Atwood, Frith, & Hermelin, 1988).

Gesture System:

greeting = high five and eye contact	yes = clap;
request for more = hand out, palm up	I'm ready = eye gaze or hand out, palm up

Baseline: 0

Progress will be reported to parents monthly and data will be collected and evaluated by SLP.

Aligns with alternative achievement standard 1 of Communication Arts of Missouri Alternative Curriculum.

Here is example goal 7 placed in a model IEP form

Instructional Area: Communication Skills
Annual Goal: Jaden will engage in communication exchanges in structured tasks by achieving the 3/3 benchmarks below: Baseline: 0/3
Aligns with alternative achievement standard 1 of Communication Arts of Missouri Alternative Curriculum
Objectives: 1. Jaden will locate device for an average of 60% of opportunities across 3 of 5 data collection days per month by locating it with faded visual cues (West, 2008). Baseline is 0% of opportunities. Qualitative cue data: Requires ___ reminders 2. Jaden will access his device for an average of 60% of opportunities across 3 of 5 data collection days per month by locating it with faded visual cues (West, 2008). Baseline is 0% of opportunities. Qualitative cue data: Requires ___ reminders 3. Jaden will demonstrate 4/4 following gestures to communicate independently in structured settings (Daniels, 1996; Atwood, Frith, & Hermelin, 1988). **Gesture System:** greeting = high five and eye contact   yes = clap; request for more = hand out, palm up   I'm ready = eye gaze or hand out, palm up Baseline: 0

REPORTING PROGRESS: the parents will be informed monthly on progress.

Oakland School District Model IEP Form (OSD, 2016)

Example Goal 8

Background: Xavier is a 2nd grade student with a diagnosis of cerebral palsy and is eligible for services in the Orthopedic Impairment category. Xavier's main mode of mobility is a wheel-chair that he can independently self-propel at slow rate up to 20 ft. lengths, which is functional for his routines and environment in the school setting. This month, he was medically cleared to begin gait training with an ambulation aid and trained adult assistants. Currently, he ambulates 6 steps (2 feet) with walker and adult holding gait belt from right (weaker) side. He verbalizes fatigue and requests a break, then refuses to walk after that point. When provided with functional motivators at the end of the gait training (using watering can for flowers, raising the school flag, opening the milk crates/ice cream freezer door, etc.), he does not verbalize fatigue.

Area of Need: Gross Motor

Annual Goal: Xavier will ambulate an average of 4 feet with gait trainer and adult assistance using a daily chore/job chart (Rossman, 2002, Weissbourd, 2014) approach to address motivation.

Data will be charted on daily chore chart and a copy will be sent home to parents weekly in Friday folder. Averages will be calculated monthly to track progress.

Baseline: 6 steps

Supports for personnel: Para educators will be trained by PT on gait belt use and walker storage/maintenance.

Aligns: Show Me Standard (Missouri) 4 of Physical Fitness and Health: "principles of movement and physical fitness."

Example Goal 9

Background: Kari is an 8th grade student with a learning disability in reading comprehension exhibiting particular difficulty with vocabulary development.

Area of Need: Reading Comprehension (Portfolio)

Annual Goal: Kari will complete semantic maps with assistance for a portfolio for 10 words per week for science and 10 words per week for social studies (instead of quizzes or tests on these words).

There will be 25 weeks of instruction included in this count. Word counts will be completed weekly by teachers and they will communicate to parents via email or weekly folder if Kari has completed her word maps.

Teachers will select the 10 words in each area and provide prompts for the semantic maps to be completed in class related to weekly topics.

At the end of the school year, Kari will present her portfolio to her teachers to demonstrate that she has met this goal.

Research: Semantic maps (Heimlich & Pittleman, 1986).

Baseline: 0- Kari has not developed any semantic maps as this is a new strategy to teach her.

Criterion to meet goal: 250 words in science and 250 words in social studies.

Aligns with ELA-Literacy RI.8.4 and RL8.4 (reading for information and reading literature) "Determine the meaning of words and phrases as they are used in the text...".

References

American Speech-Language Hearing Association, (2016). Speech sound disorders-articulation and phonology treatment practice portal [On-line]. Retrieved from ww.asha.org/ PRPSpecificTopic.aspx?folderid=85899353 21&section=Treatment

Atwood, A., Frith, U., & Hermelin, B. (1988). The understanding and use of interpersonal gestures by autistic and down's syndrome children. *Journal of Autism and Developmental Disorders 18 (2)*, 241-257.

Baker, E. (2010). Minimal Pair Intervention. In A. L. Williams, S. McLeod and R. J. McCauley (Eds.), *Interventions for Speech Sound Disorders in Children*, (pp. 41-72). Baltimore: Paul H. Brookes Publishing.

Blache, S. E., Parsons, C. L., & Humphreys, J. M. (1981). A minimal-word-pair model for teaching the linguistic significant difference of distinctive feature properties. *Journal of Speech and Hearing Disorders, 46*, 291-296.

California Department of Education (2016). *California learning frameworks for preschool* [On-line]. Retrieved from http://www.cde.ca.gov/sp/cd/re/ documents/psframeworkkvol1.pdf

Chilson, R. F. (1979). *Effects of cued speech on lip reading ability.* Master's thesis, University of Rhode Island.

Colorado Department of Elementary and Secondary Education (2016). Model IEP form [On-line]. Retrieved from http://www.cde.state.co.us/cdesped/iep_forms

Cornett, R. O. & Daisey, M. (2001). *Cued Speech. The Cued Speech resource book for parents of deaf children.* Cleveland, OH: National Cued Speech Association.

Daniels, M. (1996). Seeing language: the effect over time of sign language on vocabulary development in early childhood education. *Child Study Journal. 26 (3),* 193-208.

Doran, G.T., (1981). "There's a S.M.A.R.T. Way to Write Management Goals and Objectives", Management Review, Vol. 70, Issue 11, pp. 35-36.

Dublinske, S. (1981). Impact of EHA on speech language pathology and audiology programs in public schools. Los Angeles: University of Southern California.

Ebbels, S. (2007). Teaching grammar to school-aged children with specific language impairment using shape coding. *Child Language Teaching and Therapy 23 (1) 67-83.*

Education for All Handicapped Children Act of 1975, Pub. L. No. 94-142, § 89, et seq.

Ehren, B. (2000). Maintaining a therapeutic focus and sharing responsibility for students Success: Keys to in-class speech-language services. *Language, Speech, and Hearing Services in Schools, 31 (3). 219-300.*

Elementary and Secondary Education Act (ESEA) of 1965, Pub. L. No. 89-10, 20 U.S.C., § 2701 et seq.

Fisher, D., Frey, N., & Thousand, J. (2003). What do special educators need to know and be prepared to do for inclusive schooling to work? Teacher Education and Special Education, 26(1), 42-50.

Heimlich, J. E., and S. D. Pittelman. (1986). *Semantic Mapping: Classroom Applications.* Newark, DE: International Reading Association.

Idol, L., Nevin, A. & Paolucci-Whitcomb, P. (2000). Collaborative consultation. Austin: Pro-Ed.

Individuals with Disabilities in Education Act (IDEA) of 1990, Pub. L. No. 101-476, 20 U.S.C., § 1400 *et seq.*

Individuals with Disabilities in Education Act (IDEA) Amendments of 1997, Pub. L. No. 105- 17, (amending 20 U.S.C. § 1400 *et seq.*).

Individuals with Disabilities in Education Act (IDEA) Amendments of 2004, Pub. L. No. 105- 17, (amending 20 U.S.C. § 1400 *et seq.*).

Individuals with Disabilities in Education Act-Reauthorized Statute Summary on individualized education program of 2004. [On-line]. Retrieved from http://www2.ed.gov/ policy/speced/guid/idea/tb-iep.pdf

International Institute for Education Planning (UNESCO). (2007). Reforming school supervision for quality improvement: Module 2 Roles and functions of supervisors. [On-line]. Retrieved from http://www.unesco.org/iiep/PDF/TR_Mods/SUP_Mod2.pdf

Kaplan, H. (1974). *The effects of cued speech on the speechreading ability of the deaf.* Doctoral dissertation, University of Maryland.

Kinsella, K. Stump, S., & Feldman, K. (2000). Strategies for vocabulary development: what works. [On-line] Retrieved from http://www.phschool.com/ eteach/language_arts/2002_03/essay.html

Koegel, L., Koegel, R., & Ingham, J. (1986). Programming rapid generalization of correct articulation through self-monitoring procedures. *Journal of Speech, Language, & Hearing Disorders, 51, 24-32.*

Mitchell L., Yell, M., & Rozalski, M. (2013). The peer-reviewed requirement of the IDEA: An examination of law and policy. In Cook, Melody Tankersley, Timothy J. Landrum (Eds.), *Evidence-based practices: Advances in learning and behavioral disabilities, vol. 26* (pp.149 – 172). United Kingdom: Emerald Publishing.

Missouri Department of Elementary and Secondary Education (2013). Top indicators found out of compliance [On-line] Retrieved from http://dese.mo.gov/sites/default/files/TOP%20Indicators%Found%20OUT%20 Compliance.pdf

Missouri Department of Elementary and Secondary Education (2016). Model IEP form [On-line] Retrieved from http://dese.mo.gov/ special-education/ compliance/special-education-forms

Missouri Department of Elementary and Secondary Education (2016). Compliance and standard indicators manual [On-line]. Retrieved from http://dese.mo.gov/sites/default/files/200SpeEdProcess.pdf

No Child Left Behind Act of 2001 – US Department of Education. (n.d.). Retrieved July 30, 2016, from http://www.2.ed.gov/policy/elsec/let/ esea02/107-110.pdf

Oakland California School District. (2016). Model IEP form [On-line]. Retrieved from https://oakland.k12.mi.us/instructional/technical-assistance/

special-ed-compliance/iep-development/Documents/7a1.%20Goal%20
page%20for%20MI-Star%20IEP%202015.pdf

Office of Special Education and Rehabilitation Services (1997). *25 years of
Progress: In Educating Children with Disabilities through IDEA* [On-line].
Retrieved from https://www2.ed.gov/policy/speced/leg/idea/history.pdf

Office of Special Education and Rehabilitation Services (2014). *IDEA state de-
terminations under results driven accountability: 2014* [On-line]. Retrieved
from http://www2.ed.gov/ fund/data/report/idea/2014-chart-1.pdf

Office of Special Education and Rehabilitation Services (2015). *IDEA state deter-
minations under results driven accountability: 2015* [On-line]. Retrieved from
http://www2.ed.gov/fund/data/report/idea/2015partbrdadeterminations.pdf

Ott, K., & Wakefield, L. (2014). How to write SMARTER IEP goals: Strategies
for SLPs. [Webinar]. Retrieved from http://www.speechpathology.com/
slp-ceus/course/to-write-smarter-iep-goals-6740

Ott, K., & Wakefield, L. (2015). How to save time and develop legally compliant IEP goals [Webinar]. Retrieved from http://www.smartersteps.com

Proctor-Williams, K., & Fey, M. (2007). Recast density and acquisition of
novel irregular past tense verbs. *Language, Speech, and Hearing Services in
Schools, 50 (10). 1029-1047.*

Pudelski, S. (2016). *Executive summary of the American Association of School
Administrators* [On-line]. Retrieved from http://www.aasa.org/uploaded-
Files/Policy_and_Advocacy/Public_Policy_Resources/Special_Education/
AASARethinkingSpecialEdDueProcess.pdf

Rossman, M. (2002). Involving children in household tasks: is it worth
the effort? [On-line]. Retrieved from http://ghk.h-cdn.co/assets/

cm/15/12/55071e0298a05_-_Involving-children-in-household-tasks-U-of-M.pdf

Samuels, C. (2015). More states meet requirements under federal special education rating system. Education Week, July 15, 2015. [On-line]. Retrieved from http://blogs.edweek.org/edweek/speced/2015/07/more_states_meet_ requirements.html

Smith, C.B. (1997). Vocabulary instruction and reading comprehension: Review of the research. ERIC Digest. [On-line]. Retrieved from ww.ericdigests.org/1998-1/vocabulary.htm

Sussan, T., Greenwald, S., &Wesler, J. (2015). United states district court upholds SGW victory against summit schools [On-line]. Retrieved from http://special-ed-_law.com/blog/item/77-district-court-upholds-sgw-victory-against-summit-schools

Theisman, K., & Goldstein, H. (2001). Social stories, written text cues, and video feedback: effects on social communication of children with autism. *Journal of Applied Behavior Analysis 34 (4)*, 425-446.

United States Department of Education. (2001*). Executive summary: reauthorization of the elementary and secondary education act*, (2001). [On-line]. Retrieved from www.ed.gov/nclb/overview/intro/execsumm.html

United States Department of Education. (2004*). Building the legacy: IDEA 2004 model forms (2004)*. [On-line]. Retrieved from http://idea.ed.gov/static/modelForms

Wakefield, L. (2004). *Field notes on teacher frustrations for IEP goal collaboration.* Unpublished manuscript.

Weiner, F. (1981). Treatment of phonological disability using the method of meaningful minimal contrast: Two case studies. *Journal of Speech and Hearing Disorders, 46,* 97-103.

Weissbourd, (2014). *Executive summary: The children we mean to raise* [Online]. http://mcc.gse.harvard.edu/files/gse-mcc/files/mcc-executive-summary.pdf

West, E. (2008). Effects of verbal cues versus pictorial cues on the transfer of stimulus control for children with autism. *Focus on Autism and Other Developmental Disabilities, 23(4),* 229–241.

Whitmire, K. (2002). The evolution of school-based speech-language services: A half century of change and a new century of practice. Communication Disorders Quarterly, 23(2), 68-76.

Will, M. (1986). Educating children with learning problems: A shared responsibility. Exceptional Children, 52, 411-415.

Wolfensberger, W. (1972). The principle of normalization in human services. Toronto: National Institute on Mental Retardation.

Appendix A

Professional Development Plan

Name: School Year:

Overview

This Professional Development Plan utilizes the S.M.A.R.T.E.R. STEPS™ Guide to Creating Smarter IEP Goals.

The topic areas covered are:

a. The history of IDEA
b. Results Driven Accountability
c. The 13 Federal mandates for IEP goals
d. SMARTER Steps for IEP goals
e. Examples of SMARTER IEP goals

Learning can be demonstrated through professional reflection summaries that serve as guides for conferences with supervisors or teams. Professionals will develop a portfolio of SMARTER IEP goals of their students so that the information can be generalized into professional practice immediately. IEP teams spend a large amount of time before and after school working on IEP goals. Often, this is outside the school day or contract hours. This professional development series can assist educators with obtaining professional development credit that is meaningful. It also provides educators with practical information on legal compliance in user-friendly language. Finally, when educators are adequately trained on the legal compliance requirements, there are fewer disputes with parents. This leads to more positive student outcomes and creates a more constructive learning environment for everyone.

Instructions for How to Use the Professional Development Plan

1. Complete the **Professional Development Plan** template that follows these instructions.
2. Fill in your demographic information at the top of the form.
3. Fill in your state's quality/standard indicators that the plan will be addressing. The goals listed should align with the quality/standard indicators you have selected.
4. Fill in the due dates for your activities. Allow at least one hour for each activity.
5. This professional development series contains 5 hours of coursework. Additionally, 5-10 hours should be credited for portfolio construction time. We recommend that professionals receive one hour of contact time per student in his/her portfolio. Professionals need to have at least five students in their portfolio in order to develop a foundation of S.M.A.R.T.E.R. skill sets. The total professional development contact hours could be 15-20 hours depending on how many students are selected for the portfolio. More portfolio time can be added depending on the requirements of the professional's state or district. The portfolio should be presented in a summative conference.
6. Add any other materials or resources that you will be using in the Materials and Resources section on the Professional Development Template.
7. Fill in the information needed for the progress monitoring section.

8. Add any comments to further explain the plan. You can add comments like "See attached supporting documents," if you needed more space for comments.

9. Complete the **Professional Development Monitor Tracking Form** that follows the **Professional Development Plan.** Provide this progress-monitoring tool to your supervisor along with your Professional Development Plan. This can be used as a helpful tracking instrument to supplement other professional development rubrics that your district may use.

10. Complete the reflection pages for Chapters 1-5.

11. If you would like to customize your own professional development plan, a blank template is provided as well.

12. If you would like to customize your own reflection summary, a blank template is provided.

13. If you would like to add a self-checking comprehension quiz as part of your plan, the quiz can be found in the appendices.

 **Professional Development Plan**

Name: School Year:

Quality/Standard Indicators to be addressed:

1.

2.

Goals:

1. Review 9 stressors related to IEP goals.
2. Review 4 population targets of Results Driven Accountability.
3. Review 13 federal mandates for IEP Goal development to improve student outcomes.
4. Review 7 steps of the S.M.A.R.T.E.R. process for creating federally compliant IEP goals.
5. Develop 5 Reflective Summaries on how the information applies to my professional practice.
6. Develop S.M.A.R.T.E.R. IEP goals for _____ students on my caseload.
7.
8.
9.

Activities to accomplish goals:

1. Read Ch. 1 and complete reflection page due date:_____
2. Read Ch. 2 and complete reflection page due date:_____
3. Read Ch. 3 and complete reflection page due date:_____

4. Read Ch. 4 and complete reflection page due date:_____
5. Read Ch. 5 and complete reflection page due date:_____
6. Create a portfolio of S.M.A.R.T.E.R. IEP Goals for _____
   students. due:_____

Materials and Resources:

1. **S.M.A.R.T.E.R. STEPS™ Guide to Creating S.M.A.R.T.E.R. IEP Goals**
2. Student IEPs
3.

Progress Monitoring:

1. Reflection pages will be submitted to:_____
2. Portfolio of S.M.A.R.T.E.R. IEP goals will be submitted to:_____
3. Conference date(s):_____
4. Total Professional Development hours:_____

Comments:

Kelly Ott, MEd, MHS, CCC-SLP and Lara Wakefield, PhD, CCC-SLP

 **S.M.A.R.T.E.R.** STEPS — Professional Development Monitor Tracking Form

Name:_____ School Year:_____

Supervisor:_____ Title:_____

Resources: Guide to Creating S.M.A.R.T.E.R. IEP goals, Student IEPs

Date Submitted	Activity Number	Activity Description	Approved Yes/No	Date Approved	Supervisor's Initials	Supervisor's Comments
	1	Ch. 1 Reflection	☐ Yes ☐ No			
	2	Ch. 2 Reflection	☐ Yes ☐ No			
	3	Ch. 3 Reflection	☐ Yes ☐ No			
	4	Ch. 4 Reflection	☐ Yes ☐ No			
	5	Ch. 5 Reflection	☐ Yes ☐ No			
	6	Portfolio	☐ Yes ☐ No			
	7		☐ Yes ☐ No			
	8		☐ Yes ☐ No			
	9		☐ Yes ☐ No			
	10		☐ Yes ☐ No			

Comments:_____

_____
_____
_____
_____
_____
_____
_____
_____
_____
_____

Reflection: Guide to Creating S.M.A.R.T.E.R. Goals

Name: _____   Date: _____

Chapter One: Goal Development Stressors

Focus of Chapter (Check One):
X 9 Stressors of IEP Goals ____ 4 populations of Results Driven Accountability

___ 13 Federal Mandates for IEP Goals ____ 7 steps to S.M.A.R.T.E.R. IEP Goals

Define 3 important ideas/concepts you learned from this chapter:

1. individualized:

2. misappropriations:

3. FAPE:

Explain one idea from the chapter that will influence your professional practice:

Comments:

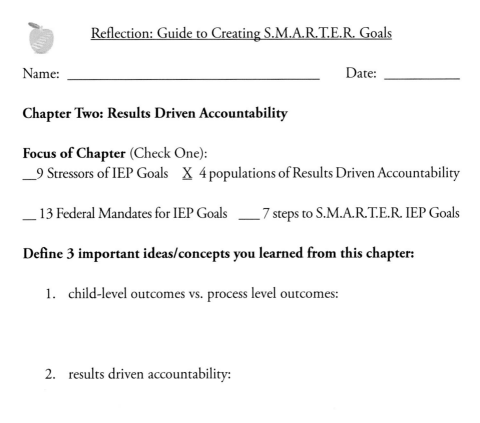

Reflection: Guide to Creating S.M.A.R.T.E.R. Goals

Name: _____ Date: _____

Chapter Two: Results Driven Accountability

Focus of Chapter (Check One):
__9 Stressors of IEP Goals   X 4 populations of Results Driven Accountability

__ 13 Federal Mandates for IEP Goals   ___ 7 steps to S.M.A.R.T.E.R. IEP Goals

Define 3 important ideas/concepts you learned from this chapter:

1. child-level outcomes vs. process level outcomes:

2. results driven accountability:

3. outcome of T.O vs Summit Schools:

Explain one idea from the chapter that will influence your professional practice:

Comments:

Reflection: Guide to Creating SMARTER Goals

Name: _____   Date: _____

Chapter Three: 13 Federal Mandates

Focus of Chapter (Check One):
___ 9 Stressors of IEP Goals   ___ 4 populations of Results Driven Accountability

X 13 Federal Mandates for IEP Goals   ___ 7 steps to S.M.A.R.T.E.R. IEP Goals

Define 3 important ideas/concepts you learned from this chapter:

1. academic, development, and functional areas of need:

2. measurability:

3. peer-reviewed research requirement:

Explain one idea from the chapter that will influence your professional practice:

Comments:

Reflection: Guide to Creating SMARTER Goals

Name: _____   Date: _____

Chapter Four: S.M.A.R.T.E.R. Steps™

Focus of Chapter (Check One):
__9 Stressors of IEP Goals ___ 4 populations of Results Driven Accountability

__ 13 Federal Mandates for IEP Goals   X 7 steps to S.M.A.R.T.E.R. IEP Goals

Define 3 important ideas/concepts you learned from this chapter:

1. specific action words:

2. evaluation and communication:

3. relevancy:

Explain one idea from the chapter that will influence your professional practice:

Comments:

Reflection: Guide to Creating SMARTER Goals

Name: _____ Date: _____

Chapter Five: S.M.A.R.T.E.R. Examples

Focus of Chapter (Check One):
___ 9 Stressors of IEP Goals ___ 4 populations of Results Driven Accountability

___ 13 Federal Mandates for IEP Goals ___ 7 steps to S.M.A.R.T.E.R. IEP Goals

X S.M.A.R.T.E.R. Goal Examples
Discuss 3 goal examples you found helpful from this chapter:

1.

2.

3.

Explain one idea from the chapter that will influence your professional practice:

Comments:

Professional Development Plan

Name: _____ School Year: _____

Quality/Standard Indicators to be addressed:

Goals:

Activities to accomplish goals:

Materials and Resources:

1.

2.

3.

4.

Progress Monitoring:

1. Reflection pages will be submitted to:_____
2. Portfolio submitted to:_____
3. Conference date(s):_____
4. Total Professional Development hours:_____

Comments:

Appendix B

"Blank Reflection Sheet" available for personal customization on the next page.

Kelly Ott, MEd, MHS, CCC-SLP and Lara Wakefield, PhD, CCC-SLP

 <u>Blank Reflection Sheet</u>

Name: Date:

Activity:

Focus of Activity (Check One):
__ Stressors of IEP Goals   ___ Results Driven Accountability

__ 13 Federal Mandates for IEP Goals   ___ S.M.A.R.T.E.R. IEP Goals

__ Other:_____

List 3 important ideas/concepts you learned from this activity:

1.

2.

3.

Explain one idea from the activity that you will influence your professional practice:

Comments:

Appendix C

<u>Professional Development Quiz</u>

Name:_____   Date:_____

1. An important distinction in the definition of "Individualized" for IEPs when developing goals is to remember:

   a. "Individualized" means that it is unique to each child and should contain customized goals and not a cookie cutter approach.
   b. "Individualized" means that goals should change from year to year because a child should be showing some kind of change in a year whether it is progression or regression.
   c. "Individualized" means that goals are data-driven based on that individual child's progress or lack of progress.
   d. all of the above

2. The purpose of developing an IEP goal is to

   a. assist the IEP team toward instruction
   b. create a situation that allows the student to do what he or she wants

    c. map out the specific steps and instruction for making academic & functional progress

    d. make it difficult to achieve within a year

3. IDEA Reauthorization 2004 brought about which important changes related to IEP goals

    a. services base on peer-reviewed research

    b. how progress will be measured

    c. when progress will be reported to parents

    d. all of the above

4. What part of the SMARTER mnemonic is addressed in the under-lined part of this IEP goal:

Joe will produce /s/ in initial position of words during reading circle and word study time with visual cues for placement and highlighted letters in books and word lists. Annual goal is <u>to achieve an average of 60% accuracy. This will be measured by one time per week checklists by teacher and SLP. Weekly totals will be averaged each month</u> and communicated to parents via email. Intervention services will be provided during reading/word study time 5 times per week for 10 minutes each as evidenced by distributed practice research (Willingham, 2002; Sexton, 2006; Kuhn, 2006; Camarata, 2010). This goal aligns with common core standards for 4th grade English Language Arts CCSS.ELA-LITERACY.SL.4.1.A.

    a. specific

    b. measurable

    c. attainable within a year

    d. teachable with strategies and cues

5. What part of the SMARTER mnemonic is addressed in the under-lined part of this IEP goal:

Joe will produce /s/ in initial position of words during reading circle and word study time with visual cues for placement and highlighted letters in books and word lists. Annual goal is to achieve an average of 60% accuracy. This will be measured by one time per week checklists by teacher and SLP. Weekly totals will be averaged each month and communicated to parents via email. <u>Intervention services will be provided during reading/word study time 5 times per week for 10 minutes each as evidenced by distributed practice research (Willingham, 2002; Sexton, 2006; Kuhn, 2006, Camarata, 2010).</u> This goal aligns with common core standards for 4th grade English Language Arts CCSS.ELA-LITERACY.SL.4.1.A.

    a.   research-based
    b.   evaluated and communicated to parents
    c.   relevant to common core or state standards
    d.   none of the above

6. What part of the SMARTER mnemonic is addressed in the under-lined part of this IEP goal:

<u>Joe will produce /s/ in initial position of words during reading circle and word study time</u> with visual cues for placement and highlighted letters in books and word lists. Annual goal is to achieve an average of 60% accuracy. This will be measured by one time per week checklists by teacher and SLP. Weekly totals will be averaged each month and communicated to parents via email. Intervention services will be provided during reading/word study time 5 times per week for 10 minutes each as evidenced by

distributed practice research (Willingham, 2002; Sexton, 2006; Kuhn, 2006; Camarata, 2010). This goal aligns with common core standards for 4th grade English Language Arts CCSS.ELA-LITERACY.SL.4.1.A.

a. specific
b. measurable
c. attainable within a year
d. none of the above

7. What part of the SMARTER mnemonic is addressed in the underlined part of this IEP goal:

Joe will produce /s/ in initial position of words during reading circle and word study time with visual cues for placement and highlighted letters in books and word lists. Annual goal is to achieve an average of 60% accuracy. This will be measured by one time per week checklists by teacher and SLP. Weekly totals will be averaged each month and communicated to parents via email. Intervention services will be provided during reading/word study time 5 times per week for 10 minutes each as evidenced by distributed practice research (Willingham, 2002; Sexton, 2006; Kuhn, 2006; Camarata, 2010). <u>This goal aligns with common core standards for 4th grade English Language Arts CCSS.ELA-LITERACY.SL.4.1.A: "Engage effectively in a range of collaborative discussions (one-on-one, in groups, and teacher-led) with diverse partners on grade 4 topics and texts, building on others' ideas and expressing their own clearly."</u>

a. research-based
b. evaluated and communicated to parents
c. relevant to common core or state standards
d. none of the above

8. What part of the SMARTER mnemonic is addressed in the under-
lined part of this IEP goal:

Joe will produce /s/ in initial position of words during reading
circle and word study time with visual cues for placement and
highlighted letters in books and word lists. Annual goal is to
achieve an average of 60% accuracy. This will be measured by
one time per week checklists by teacher and SLP. <u>Weekly totals
will be averaged each month and communicated to parents via
email.</u> Intervention services will be provided during reading/word
study time 5 times per week for 10 minutes each as evidenced by
distributed practice research (Willingham, 2002; Sexton, 2006;
Kuhn, 2006; Camarata, 2010). This goal aligns with common
core standards for 4th grade English Language Arts CCSS.ELA-
LITERACY.SL.4.1.A.

    a.   research-based
    b.   evaluated and communicated to parents
    c.   relevant to common core or state standards
    d.   none of the above

9. What part of the SMARTER mnemonic is addressed in the under-
lined part of this IEP goal:

Joe will produce /s/ in initial position of words during reading circle
and word study time <u>with visual cues for placement and highlighted letters in books and word lists</u>. Annual goal is to achieve an average of 60% accuracy. This will be measured by one time per week
checklists by teacher and SLP. Weekly totals will be averaged each
month and communicated to parents via email. Intervention services will be provided during reading/word study time 5 times per
week for 10 minutes each as evidenced by distributed practice research (Willingham, 2002; Sexton, 2006; Kuhn, 2006; Camarata,

2010). This goal aligns with common core standards for 4th grade English Language Arts CCSS.ELA-LITERACY.SL.4.1.A.

a. specific
b. measurable
c. attainable within a year
d. teachable with strategies and cues

10. What part of the SMARTER mnemonic <u>is missing</u> in the following goal:

Danielle will identify correct irregular past tense verbs in her English and Social Studies texts with an increase of average accuracy above current baseline of 40% by the end of the school year. Teachers and SLPs will use contextual recast cues during instruction and structured conversation (Nelson et. al., 1996) in distributed practice 3 times per week for 10 minutes. This goal is designed to support common core standards CCSS.ELA-LITERACY.SL.6.1.C: Pose and respond to specific questions with elaboration and detail by making comments that contribute to the topic, text, or issue under discussion.

a. attainable within a year
b. teachable with strategies and cues
c. evaluated and communicated to parents
d. specific

11. The IDEA (formerly known as EHA) was originally drafted by:

a. United States Department of Education
b. mothers of children with special needs
c. American Task Force on Special Education
d. teachers Education Agency

12. After IDEA was passed into law, university programs developed:

    a. free legal advisement programs to parents of children with special needs

    b. course catalogs in Braille

    c. ASL courses for foreign language requirement

    d. degree programs for special education teachers

13. What university was the first to offer a special education degree program?

    a. University of Iowa

    b. University of Missouri

    c. University of Illinois

    d. University of Southern California

14. The IDEA is intended to protect:

    a. graduation guarantees for students with disabilities

    b. minimum wage increases for people with disabilities

    c. civil rights of students with disabilities aged 3-21 years

    d. social security benefits of students with disabilities until age 18

15. The overall point of the IDEA is:

    a. children with disabilities have a right to a free appropriate public education similar to non-disabled children.

    b. children with disabilities can access special services at their school for a fee.

    c. children with disabilities will be educated in a separate facility than non-disabled peers.

    d. All of the above

16. What group has historically driven the special education process and are the strongest advocates for children with special needs?

    a.   special education teachers
    b.   school administrators
    c.   parents of children with special needs
    d.   Teacher Education Agency

17. Best practices allow IEP teams to:

    a.   block adequate time in their schedules for collaborative goal planning
    b.   allow time for data tracking and progress monitoring
    c.   create individualized goals for each student
    d.   all of the above

18. Misappropriation funds refers to:

    a.   sharing funding for students across school districts
    b.   denying a funding request for a football field
    c.   spending earmarked funds for one program on a different program
    d.   none of the above

19. Emotional capital refers to

    a.   feelings, beliefs, and energy that an IEP team invests in a student
    b.   funds spent on emotional intelligence training
    c.   psychological diagnoses that cost the school district money
    d.   funding for counseling programs

20. The federal government provides what percentage of funding to special education programs?

    a. 20%
    b. 30%
    c. 40%
    d. 50%

21. A framework that is designed to assess how states are showing progress with students of 4 target populations is called:

    a. Office of Special Education and Rehabilitation Services
    b. Results Driven Accountability
    c. United States Department of Education
    d. Association of School Administrators

22. If a state does not meet the requirements of the RDA rubric, the IDEA mandates that the state will need to take specific actions such as:

    a. prepare a corrective action plan
    b. enter into a compliance agreement
    c. limit state's funding
    d. all of the above

23. Which of the following groups is NOT a target population for the RDA rubric:

    a. preschoolers
    b. fifth graders
    c. transition age students 16 years and older
    d. high school graduates who had IEPs

24. IEP goals must address:

    a.   academic needs of the student
    b.   developmental needs of the student
    c.   functional needs of the student
    d.   all of the above

25. IEP goals must document progress by demonstrating:

    a.   they are measurable with baselines, data collection, and mastery levels
    b.   they are written on graph paper
    c.   they are created in a spreadsheet
    d.   they are plotted on a bell curve

Answer Key

  1. d
  2. c
  3. d
  4. b
  5. a
  6. a
  7. c
  8. b
  9. d
10. c
11. b
12. d
13. c
14. c
15. a

16. c
17. d
18. c
19. a
20. c
21. b
22. d
23. b
24. d
25. a

Appendix D

"S.M.A.R.T.E.R. STEPS Goal Worksheet" available for reproduction on the next page.

Kelly Ott, MEd, MHS, CCC-SLP and Lara Wakefield, PhD, CCC-SLP

S.M.A.R.T.E.R. STEPS™ Goal Worksheet

Student Name:_____Grade:_____Class:_____

Specific Skills	Action Words
1._____	1._____
2._____	2._____
3._____	3._____
4._____	4._____
5._____	5._____
Measurement Options	Data Collection/Baseline
1._____	1._____
2._____	2._____
3._____	3._____
4._____	4._____
5._____	5._____
Teachable Prompts & Strategies	Research/Evidence
1._____	1._____
2._____	2._____
3._____	3._____
4._____	4._____
5._____	5._____

Appendix E

"S.M.A.R.T.E.R. STEPS Goal Template" available for reproduction on the next page.

Kelly Ott, MEd, MHS, CCC-SLP and Lara Wakefield, PhD, CCC-SLP

S.M.A.R.T.E.R. STEPS™ Goal Template

Student:_____ Grade:_____
School:_____ School Year:_____ Date:_____

S	Specific skill set and observable behaviors; use specific action words, contexts, & settings	
M	Measurable with meaningful and manageable data collection, including baselines	
A	Attainable within an annual IEP cycle	
R	Research/Evidence based instructional methods that are documented within the goal	
T	Teachable with cues and strategies that are explained in the goal	
E	Evaluate data & communicate regularly to parents	
R	Relevant to general education curriculum or state standards	

Appendix F

"Prioritization Worksheet" available for reproduction on the next page.

Kelly Ott, MEd, MHS, CCC-SLP and Lara Wakefield, PhD, CCC-SLP

Prioritization Worksheet

Student's Name: _____ Date: _____

Team Concerns	Area of Need	Priority Code

Areas to Address in this IEP Cycle		Person to Collect Data

Areas of Concern to Address in the future		Priority Code

Priority Codes:

1 Safety	3. Communication	5. Writing	7. Social
2 Behavior/Emotion	4. Reading	6. Math	8. Other

Appendix G

Model Form Research Summary

P art B of IDEA required the U.S. Department of Education to publish and widely disseminate model forms that contained all of these mandates (IDEA, 2004). The IDEA required states and local districts to develop model IEP forms to include all federal mandates. These forms are supposed to be a guide to prompt IEP teams to ensure that all requirements are met. After these model forms were developed and disseminated, there were three main problems noticed with them related to the IEP goals:

1. Information about what is supposed to be in the forms was discussed in a narrative format in the IDEA (2004) and this is difficult to translate to a one-page goal form.
2. Multiple requirements made it challenging to incorporate everything into a goal page with clear wording.
3. Redundancy of the requirements created confusion of what to enter on a form.

This is in large part, the motivation for our current review of state model forms and federal mandates surrounding IEP goal development. It is imperative to understand what is needed in our documentation so that we can demonstrate accountability in the services we provide.

It is highly recommended that you review your own state's model forms. Go to your state department of education's website and look at the model IEP forms there. Also, review your district's IEP forms and match them up to the federal requirements to determine if there are any mandates omitted.

Here is an excerpt from the Missouri Compliance Manual for IEP goals (MO DESE, 2016). Missouri was one of the green states on the OSERS compliance maps for 2014 and 2015 (RDA Summary 2014, 2015). Each compliance standard is listed and described on the state's department of education website.

200-Special Education Process

200.810 a-Demonstrate consistency with the content of PLAAFP

200.810 b-Are written in terms that are:

200.810b (1) Specific to a particular skill or behavior to be achieved

200.810b (2) Measurable

200.810b (3) Attainable (accomplished within duration of IEP)

200.810b (4) Results Oriented

200.810b (5) Time-bound (within a year)

200.810c Enable child to be involved in general education curriculum

200.810d Address child's other educational needs due to disability

200.810e Are present for each special education AND related service

200.810f Must have benchmarks for children taking Alternative Assessments

200.820 Documentation includes a statement of the special education services based on peer reviewed research (including related services)

You will notice this is where we have the beginnings of the S.M.A.R.T.E.R.™ acronym embedded into a compliance regulation. The MO DESE has recognized that they need to have some way of communicating the law into understandable terms. We have expanded this acronym to S.M.A.R.T.E.R.™ to include all 13 mandates.

After reviewing the compliance manual, the Missouri model form was reviewed. Specifically, we wanted to know "What was missing on the Missouri model form?" Here is a list of what was missing:

- no prompt for baseline performance to be recorded
- no prompt for communication to parents
- no prompt to document the research or evidence base
- no prompt for setting/context
- no prompt for goal aligning to the curriculum

State Model Forms

How can we review the model forms to know if they have everything they are supposed to have? Since the mandates contain complicated information to remember and review, we used the S.M.A.R.T.E.R.™ process to evaluate 10 states' model forms. When we visited the states' model forms on their websites, we were specifically looking at their IEP goal pages. Only two out of the ten states sampled included all 13 federal mandate prompts. This demonstrates the risk you take if you blindly assume that your state form covers all 13 mandates. We have found that claiming plausible deniability will not protect your license or standing within a school district if a child complaint is filed with your state department. It is each professional's responsibility to know and follow all mandates pertaining to special education law.

In addition to all of the federal guidelines mentioned, states and districts may have other goal requirements to add to the model forms. For example, California requires more specialized consideration for students who are English Language Learners. The federal law simply states, "The native language needs to be considered when developing the IEP" (IDEA, 2004). Also, there are districts that may receive special funds from taxpayer incentives in the county that require certain statement be documented in the IEP goals. It is important to educate yourselves about any local regulations that may apply.

Key Terms

AASA	American Association of School Administrators
Accountability	The act of being responsible for something.
ALJ	An administrative law judge presides over trials and adjudicates the claims or disputes involving administrative law.
National Center on	NCSI helps states transform their systems to
Systemic Improvement	improve outcomes for infants, toddlers, children, and youth with disabilities.
Compliance Standards	Set of rules, guidelines, and laws to be followed
DOE	Department of Education is the agency that establishes policy for, administrates, and coordinates federal and state assistance to education. There is a US DOE and each state has a DOE.

Due Process Hearing	A hearing to determine the administration of justice and fair treatment. In special education, a due process hearing is typically related to disputes over a student with disabilities receiving a free appropriate public education (FAPE).
Emotional Capital	The feelings, beliefs, perceptions and values that people hold when they engage with any business, company, or institution.
ESEA	Elementary and Secondary Education Act was passed as part of Lyndon B. Johnson's "War on Poverty" in 1965 and has been the most far reaching legislation effecting education in the U.S. The most current version of the law was updated in 2016. It is known as the "Every Student Succeeds Act" (ESSA) and replaced the previous NCLB (2002).
EBP	Evidence-based practices refer to those practices that are deemed effective through current empirical research, professional experience, and student/family values and preferences.
FAPE	Free Appropriate Public Education is an educational right of children with disabilities in the U.S. that is guaranteed by the Rehabilitation Act of 1973 and the Individuals

	with Disabilities Education Act (IDEA).
IDEA	The Individuals with Disabilities Education Act is a four-part legislation aimed at insuring children with disabilities receive a free appropriate public education that is tailored to their individual needs.
IEP	Individual Education Program is a written plan detailing the special education services, supplemental supports, accommodations, and modifications that student needs to receive a free appropriate public education.
Individualized	Specifically tailored to meet that person's unique strengths and learning needs.
Mandates	A legal requirement, not optional, must be followed.
Misappropriations	The illegal use of funds designated for a specific program for someone's own personal use or unauthorized purpose.
NCLB	No Child Left Behind was the short name of the Elementary and Secondary Education Act Reauthorization of 2002. It implemented a high-stakes testing requirement and mandated peer-reviewed research methods for students.
OSERS	Office of Special Education and Rehabilitative Services is a

program of the U.S. Department of Education that provides support to parents and individuals, school districts, and states in three main areas: special education, vocational rehabilitation, and research.

Plan A detailed proposal such as a list of activities or steps in a lesson.

Plausible deniability The ability of a person to deny knowledge or responsibility for any damnable actions committed.

Program A planned series of future events, items, or performances that is time bound and results oriented.

Related services providers Support service professionals that assist students with special needs. These may include but are not limited to speech language pathologist, occupational therapist, physical therapist, nurse, counselor, audiologist, early identification providers, nutritionist, recreation therapist, applied behavioral analyst, etc.

RDA Results-Driven Accountability is the U.S. Department of Education's new framework intended to improve educational results and functional outcomes for students with special needs.